Reflection Time

This book is dedicated
to the memory of Liz Winwood.

Reflection Time

Developing a reflective approach
to teaching and learning

Linda White

The National Society
*Leading Education
with a Christian Purpose*
Church House Publishing

National Society/Church House Publishing
Church House
Great Smith Street
London SW1P 3NZ

ISBN 0 7151 4936 9

Published 2000 by the National Society (Church of England) for Promoting Religious Education and Church House Publishing.

Cover design by Leigh Hurlock

Printed in England by The Cromwell Press Ltd, Trowbridge, Wiltshire

Contents

Acknowledgements

I would like to thank all of my family and friends, particularly Cara and Emma, who have been so supportive during the time it has taken to put this book together. I promise that I will never mention it again, Phil! Thank you to Carl and Walid for the technical advice and many thanks go to Claire Nelson for her patient support and impressive technological skills. Thank you to Collette Shaw, Emma White and Michelle Barlow for their artistic contributions. Thank you Professor John West-Burnham for encouraging me write about reflection. Thank you to the National Society for funding the research project and to Hamish Bruce and Alan Brown for their guidance. Many thanks of course go to the head teacher, staff, governors, families and children of Eastwood Infant and Nursery school in Nottinghamshire, without whom this book would not have been possible. Last but not least, thank you Class 4 – you taught me so much!

Introduction

In May 1998 I was awarded the National Society's first Special Educational Needs Research Fellowship. This book tells the story of the action research project, which was undertaken during the course of the Fellowship year, 1998-9. The project involved one class of Year 2 and Year 1 children and some of the staff of an urban infant school in the East Midlands. The book is set against a background of a government drive to raise standards, recover achievement, set targets and inspect schools, all of which are potential areas of stress not only for the adult workers but also for the children in our schools. I use the term 'workers' as opposed to teachers in recognition of the fact that many classrooms contain teams of workers, including special needs support assistants, nursery nurses, support agency workers and parents who come into contact with children during the course of the school day. The aim of the research project was to provide evidence to support the view that the development of positive, reflective relationships with very difficult or withdrawn children can in turn lead to a better self-esteem for children and adults and an improvement in the quality of learning for all.

The premise of this book is that there are many pressures on children, workers and teachers who tend to spend a great deal of time together in the same environment, which is often a confined space, for long periods of time. This situation can cause stress and the book aims to explain the development of a reflective approach to teaching and learning which has been designed to deal with stressful situations. It also explores the connections between this approach and the development of suitable learning behaviour. It aims to offer a realistic collection of practical strategies and a programme of development which is suitable for use in any busy, demanding classroom situation where the children may have difficulties listening, cooperating and staying on task. Such strategies are aimed at saving workers valuable time, which is often lost as a result of dealing with disruptive and challenging behaviour. Starting points are also offered for the teaching of religious education to very young children, whilst also focusing on their language and emotional needs and their emerging spirituality. The book considers the importance of the whole learning environment, including the practical layout of the classroom combined with the subtle features that create ethos and atmosphere.

In Part One I have described the development of a 'reflection time' as part of a reflective approach to teaching and learning. Chapter 1 sets out reasons for incorporating this reflection time into the school day. The theme is continued in Chapter 2, which describes the benefits of a reflective approach, and Chapter 3 sets the scene for a reflection time, which is described in greater detail in Chapter 4. Chapter 5 moves the reflective approach into a wider educational setting, with Chapter 6 focusing on the issues that affect schools and their workers. Chapter 7 focuses specifically on special educational needs and describes how a reflective approach is also an inclusive approach; this chapter also contains five case studies. Part Two concentrates on links with curriculum areas and Chapter 8 includes strategies for the teaching of religious education to young children. Chapter 9 considers staff development issues, including a case study, and Chapter 10 contains an evaluation and conclusion. The appendices include a description of the background to the action research project and the project school. A book list is included for further reading and a list of music is provided for use at reflection time. Appendix 4 describes the results of a drama project, which was formed on children's development in global education.

The results of the research project have lead to the definition of a development programme which according to the research material appears to be attractive to both adults and children. The reflective approach adopted by the class team involved all of the class and not just the children who were displaying difficult or demanding behaviour and it also began to affect children and staff throughout the school.

NOTE

The author and publisher gratefully acknowledge permission to reproduce the children's quoted material in this publication. Their words have been reproduced in their original form. The children use the word 'scrappy' to describe the behaviour of those children who are uncooperative, violent or generally disruptive.

The names of all children interviewed have been changed.

PART ONE

Reflection

Chapter 1

Why do reflection?

Children's thinking

In the introduction to his book about children and their thinking, Fisher (1990) states that 'the teaching of thinking skills is potentially one of the most valuable areas of educational research and development'. I agree with Fisher when he states that the foundation for thinking skills needs to be laid early in life, beginning in the formative years when a child's identity as a thinking person is being established. Although the author understands that children need to discover themselves as thinking, feeling, whole people and that they need to be given opportunities to work out their own thoughts, put ideas into words, advance theories and justify their beliefs, he accepts that the problem lies in how to do this. I found that the development of a reflection time comes close to solving this problem. It is important that thinking skills are developed in schools; however, time is not usually specifically allocated in curriculum audits for the provision of experiences that allow the use of thinking to develop high-order skills. Fisher (1990, p. 139) supports the provision of time out to think and he believes that it should be the slogan of all schools. He maintains that: 'Children need to invest more time and energy in recognising and defining problems, to inhibit their first thoughts and impulses and to take a more reflective and cautious approach.' I have found that the benefits of an approach that promotes self-control are multifarious, and as Fisher says: 'The way self-control is mediated can help to enhance cognitive development.'

Achievement

I have found that reflection time has a number of uses within the classroom situation and within a whole school context. Through reflection time I discovered that it is possible to begin to teach children to have respect for themselves and each other as well as diverse lifestyles and cultures and different religions. It is also possible to focus on the development of listening skills, which are an essential element in raising achievement and standards across the whole curriculum. All reflection times begin with music; therefore it has proved to be useful as a way of introducing children to music from around the world. Reflection time has provided a pathway for inclusion for all children and particularly those children with emotional and behavioural difficulties.

> When Neil first didn't do reflection he was all scrappy and Ryan is his mentor and when he fetched him down to do reflection it stopped him from being scrappy and when he looked round at everybody he saw them sitting nicely, he started sitting nicely and when he done reflection he was sitting in a listening position and in this class.

Lisa

> When Billy came into the class he was scrappy, when I saw him looking at the candle he was listening, and I know why reflection stopped him because he thought about how you behave.

Garry

Reflection time provides a way of teaching a form of relaxation in an increasingly stressful educational world. It is also a way to develop problem-solving and decision-making skills in very young children who may have problems communicating and who are used to expressing themselves through more physical and aggressive ways.

Feelings of calm

I initially introduced the reflection process into my classroom in order to try to meet some of the needs of some of my children. A minority of the children were finding cooperative behaviour to be difficult and one child in particular was extremely violent and in distress. Another child was finding settling into school very stressful, and many of the children were struggling with developing the language needed to achieve within the context of the National Curriculum. It was very much a response to the special needs of children and not to any directive to raise standards or to meet a quotient of expected attainment levels. The process lead to a communal feeling of calm within the classroom, which in turn made the learning process more effective for the children in the class. Some of the children were becoming tired of frequent and sometimes violent interruptions to their education; they were not having the opportunities to learn in a suitable environment. This was all taking place within the wider context of significant political and educational change. Teachers were under a great deal of stress as they responded to the increasing demands of a wider curriculum base, more complicated assessment procedures and the ever-looming threat of inspection. This pressure was also reaching the children; therefore there was a need for a 'stress-busting' tool for all of the classroom workers. Certain resources were to play an important part in developing this new approach to coping with life. Music was vital to the success of the process. I had always used music in my teaching and I had already acknowledged the many benefits of using certain music to affect behaviour, mood and learning. It had also provided the basis for discussion about various issues and lifestyles.

> Before you have reflection you have to sit properly and put some music on that you know you're gonna be all right with because at reflection if you didn't have the right type of music you couldn't do it properly, because you won't be able to sit properly and you won't have any good listening skills if you don't have the right type of music.

Zara

Candles came next; candles are always an attention stealer where young children are concerned, you just have to observe the huge pleasure and excitement induced by the ritual lighting of the birthday candles. Children also tend to become calm and respectful around candles. I had noticed this during visits to places of worship and during assembly times. Music and candles were then combined to become the 'tools of reflection'. Through the use of these tools I wanted to create a space and a calm time within which children would be left alone, not physically of course, but alone in the sense of nothing being directly asked of them other than to sit and to listen.

When we do reflection you need to make sure there's not much noise that you don't want.

Louise

I like reflection because you sit nicely and close your eyes and I like it.

Kirk

All that was required of the children was that they sit around a candle, listen to music and think; although I accept that this is not always an easy goal to achieve with some groups of children. It is important to the success of reflection time that the situation is thought through carefully beforehand. It is vital that the children are involved in discussions about the aims of reflection from the very beginning. The procedures are simple, yet the potential for learning is immense.

Difficulties children experienced

Many of the children in the class were experiencing difficulties in making progress for a variety of reasons. Some of the class had experience of death, loss and separation. One child was experiencing racial abuse. Some of the children were experiencing moderate and severe learning difficulties; some children were experiencing emotional distress, for instance one child had recently witnessed his father's fatal heart attack, and another had also experienced the loss of her father during the previous year. Some of the learning difficulties experienced by the children were connected to severe speech difficulties, and one group of children was also exhibiting a range of emotional and behavioural difficulties. One child in particular had a history of violent behaviour combined with learning problems; his extreme violence had led to his exclusion from school on a number of occasions. An approach was required to meet this child's needs, and as McNamara and Moreton (1995, p. 16) have found, children who are damaged need a therapeutic approach as punishments and sanctions are inappropriate for their needs. Also many of the children to a lesser extent found it difficult to remain on task for very long or to actually discuss any of the work they had undertaken.

When we have reflection we have time to think for our work and when we come to our work we do it straight away.

Lisa

Some children lacked the self-confidence to participate in any small or large group situation without feeling uncomfortable. The project school was basically a monocultural school, although at times children from ethnic minority backgrounds joined the school. At the time of the project, one child arrived at the school from an inner city school 10 miles away. His mother was white and his father was black and he was experiencing difficulties becoming part of a school community which was white. This child began to display aggressive and unsettled behaviour and it would appear from the research that reflection time became a way for him to cope with what was happening for him both at school and at home. He tells his own story later in the book.

Chapter 2

The benefits of using the reflective approach

One of the benefits of using a reflective approach is the high priority it gives to the development of speaking and listening skills. Good speaking and listening skills are essential to development in all areas of learning. However, it may be the case that emphasis on ways to develop these skills has been marginalized in the race to manage time audits and ensure a detailed curriculum content. Other benefits of the reflective approach are to be found in the areas of general language development and behaviour modification. Inclusion is currently high on the current educational agenda and I feel that using a reflective approach enables children, and particularly children with special educational needs, to be included in the education process.

I have found that there are some connections between teaching styles and behavioural difficulties. As McNamara and Moreton (1995, p. 17) demonstrate: 'a positive attitude from teachers towards emotionally and behaviourally disturbed pupils is vital if they are to support their pupils in their attempts to change their behaviour'. I also believe that as adults we are sometimes very unrealistic about what we expect from children. I feel that we are not always good at explaining to children what exactly we expect from them in terms of 'good' or acceptable behaviour. I have found that as a teacher I sometimes do not have the same understanding of language as the children and therefore it is important to invest some time in explaining what I mean by acceptable and unacceptable behaviour. It is not surprising that some children act as they do and become confused by the wealth of different standards of behaviour that surround them during the course of the day, both at home and at school. If a child has low self-esteem, which is reinforced throughout the day, then potentially difficult and unacceptable behaviour is likely to follow. This places a huge responsibility on the shoulders of both the school and the teacher. A reflective approach, which is based on a continuous drive to raise self-esteem, can be effective in raising standards of behaviour. This area of self-esteem is a complicated one and one which I struggle to understand. I am not an expert in this area but my experience tells me it is important to focus on specific targets for certain children as opposed to generally saying 'nice' things to children. This is particularly the case for children who are finding life in school extremely difficult to cope with. The special needs team, including the special educational needs coordinator, learning support assistants and class teacher, need to work together on consistent approaches to the use of individual education plans in order to support these children.

Teaching religious education

The reflective approach also offers a means of creating a suitable learning environment for the teaching of religious education and a pathway to a deeper exploration of the meaning of cultural, social, spiritual and moral development. I suppose that this is quite a claim for one approach to teaching and learning; however, the emphasis is on an approach which is very child-centred and has the autonomous child at its core. It is an approach that allows time for children to think and to contemplate, whilst recognizing the importance of the acquisition of relevant knowledge and the development of appropriate skills and attitudes. This kind of approach focuses on enabling children to reflect on their learning and emotional experiences and feelings, as opposed to the more traditional approach, which places curriculum knowledge and content at its centre. Hay and Nye (1998, pp. 174–5) talk about the danger of the perception that the learning of factual infor-mation about a culture is the first task of spiritual education. They believe that this can lead to a situation where the culture is divorced from the 'down–to–earth' experience. The authors fear that poorly executed approaches to religious education which 'undertake an externalised study of var-ious dimensions of religious activity (ritual, mythology, doctrine, ethics and social practice)' actually make them too distant from children's personal lives. Religious education is important for all children whatever their religious background because they need to understand that they 'are exploring aspects of a universal quest, in which they are all engaged by virtue of being human'. I have found evidence that the children enjoy and learn from the reflective approach and I feel that adults can also learn from the situation. During reflection time the children are gathered around a candle to help them to focus, which in itself is quite a spiritual setting. There is a feeling of togetherness, which could be compared with the shared experience people describe when par-ticipating in celebration or prayer in a place of worship. The sense of global feeling is enhanced through the music, which is often of 'spiritual type', and/or from different parts of the world. The behaviour modification comes from the nature of the experience, which calms children down and gives them valuable time out. Reflection time can help them to think about their actions and the effect these actions have on others. The subject of religious education is difficult to teach to young children, particularly when teaching about world religions in a monocultural situation. In this case the resources can seem very remote to children who often have no personal context in which to place these new learning experiences.

Values and attitudes

Despite the religious connections, the reflection experience does not have to have entirely religious connotations. It also provides a means for exploring values and attitudes, which are sometimes more of a moral nature. The use of reflection time can often set the scene to aid understanding of difficult issues. Reflection has a major role to play in moral education, although it needs to be linked to the practice of moral habits. Damon and Colby (1996, pp. 33–4) have found that 'both habit and reflection can be sources of moral action'. Among moral educators there has been disagreement about approaches to moral development with children, with some writers arguing that training children to have moral habits is more important that encouraging the development of moral reasoning and reflection. Damon and Colby (1996) argue against the polarization of either approach. 'The heart of moral growth is not simply acquiring good habits *or* insightful reflectiveness, rather it is developing the capacity to move easily between the two.' Reflection time offers an opportunity for the child who never usually joins in to become more involved. I have found that children who rarely make contributions to discussions feel comfortable enough to make contributions at this particular time. In my current class it took one child almost the whole of the academic year to volunteer any comment; when it did come, it came at reflection time, much to the great pleasure of all of the other children in the class, who burst into spontaneous applause. Many of our children are in pain as a result of their life experiences and the pain experienced by those around them. Consider the case of one of the children in the research project. Her father had died during the previous year and she never talked about this in school, although she did talk about her grandparent dying. When another child in school lost her father this child wrote her a note saying that she knew how the girl was feeling and that if she ever needed to talk about her daddy dying that she should come to her as she knew exactly how she must be feeling. She later told me that as a result of counselling she felt able to talk about her father's death and the reason why she had not spoken about it sooner was that she did not want her mother to suffer any more pain. The child was five when her father died and she was unable to talk about it until she was seven and had had counselling for a year.

Mentoring

Many of the major difficulties we had been experiencing in terms of behaviour in our school had involved boys who displayed disruptive and aggressive behaviour. Each year as children moved from our school, an infant school, to the junior school, another group of boys emerged displaying the same behavioural tendencies. It is often tempting to give attention to those children who are loud and aggressive and to forget about the quiet and withdrawn sort of child. As Kenway and Fitzclarence (1997, pp.122–8) have discovered as a result of their research into masculinity, violence and schooling, there is an argument that for boys who are marginalized educationally and socially disadvantaged, 'risky and violent behaviour provides almost the only way of obtaining status and cultural resources'. They do also admit that it is unclear how schools might

effectively address these complex issues. However, they do advocate more of a reflective institutional approach and less of an individual pathological view of the problem in schools, which tend to blame peer groups, families or media for violence in schools and beyond. They recommend that the institution needs to look at itself as it may be colluding in the acceptance of violence in deeper ways. The authors agree that there needs to be a greater emphasis placed on emotional development in schools because 'to ignore the emotional world of schooling and of students and teachers is to contribute to the repressions which recycle and legitimate violence'. Some boys display different types of learning needs and an awareness of this helps when analysing what is going on in the area of behaviour both within the classroom and out in the playground. To address some of these learning needs I introduced a dance project and a mentoring project. After a great deal of discussion with the children, about both of the projects, it was decided that certain children would become mentors. I initially introduced the concept of mentoring to the project class and as younger boys from another class were sent to the project class for 'time out', it naturally evolved that some of the children (mainly boys) took on the role of mentor for these children. The effect that the mentoring system had on behaviour is discussed in greater detail in the case study section in Chapter 7. I believe that the mentoring system had a positive effect on the children's behaviour; however, we all worked together to deal with situations and problems as they presented themselves. The children also believed that mentoring was a 'good thing to do', and they seemed to have grasped the basic idea of the mentor's role.

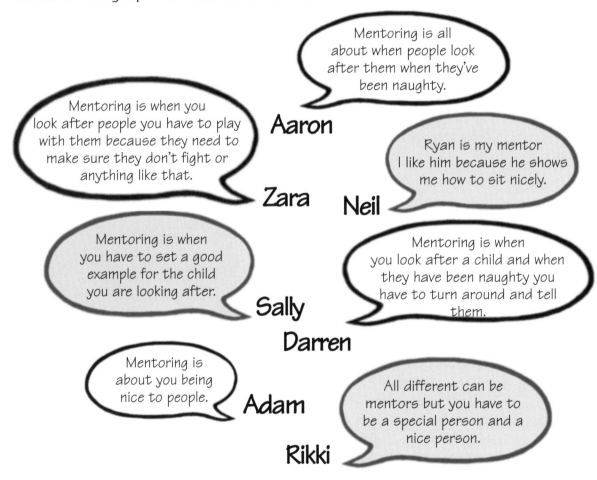

Some children developed long-term mentoring relationships, although they weren't always easy relationships. If children became overzealous in their duties as mentors then this would be a situation which would require a measure of adult intervention. This was also the case if the mentoring role became too consuming and intruded on the mentor's time; however, I found that the advantages outweighed the disadvantages. A system does need to be monitored and if the relationships aren't working then modifications need to be made to match individual situations.

refletion is all About when yo sit in A circle and what the day has been Like and Im A mentor and A mentor is when you help people who are Not Listening To the Teacher to pay Attention.

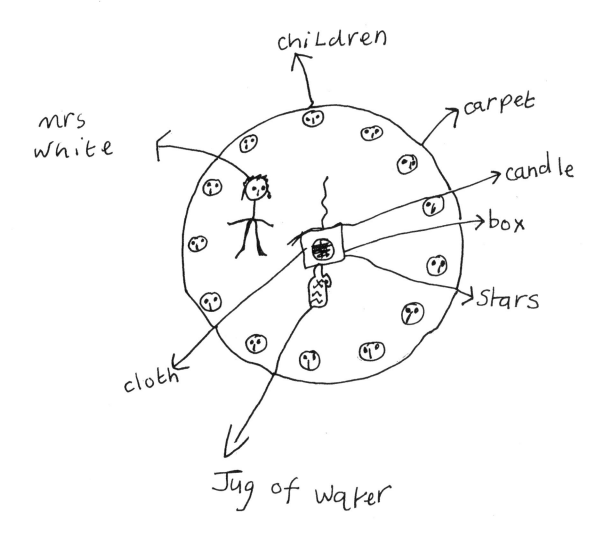

mrs white

children

carpet

candle

box

Stars

cloth

Jug of water

Chapter 3

Setting the scene for reflection time

Attitude

A belief that a reflective approach can work is a necessary component for a successful reflection time. Having an open mind and giving this type of approach time to work, modifying it to meet the needs of the group or the age of the children or the type of school conditions that exist, is also essential. It definitely takes time to involve all of the group; I have found that I slightly alter the scenario as my class make-up changes with a new intake, or if I find that one particular group responds to certain music or time of day for instance. It is important to keep the children involved by asking their opinions and finding out afterwards what their reaction is. The most vital aspect is to hand over the time to them and not to put pressure on them by insisting they react at the end of the session as if had been a lesson.

> When you do reflection you need a nice calm classroom with pictures and stuff around it and calm music and a nice candle and when you look at the candle flame it makes you think you're on the beach as the sun is setting.
>
> **Sally**

> I like reflection because it makes you calm and everyone looks at the candle with their
>
> **Zara**

If the process has been carefully thought out and planned for before the session begins, it will avoid any negative interruptions, which usually destroy the atmosphere.

Setting the scene

It is very important at this stage to 'set the scene' because if time and attention are not given to this point then the whole experience could be devalued. It is crucial to create a relevant atmosphere to induce the feeling that something special is taking place or is about to take place.

> When we first start reflection, you've got to wait till everyone sits down and doesn't move and sit in the listening position.
>
> **Zara**

This includes making sure that the session is not interrupted: this is not always an easy situation to guarantee in the primary school situation. I have found that a 'DO NOT DISTURB' sign is a necessary visual aid for these purposes. It is also so important to help the teacher and the children to feel comfortable. I have found that adopting something called the 'listening position' is beneficial.

This probably sounds strange at first but it is a little body language invention that works and does prevent the usual small fingers wandering into the Lego or adopting the professional stance of a hairdresser. The listening position is where the children sit cross-legged with the palms of their hands facing upwards and resting on their knees.

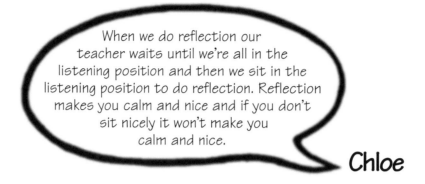

When we do reflection our teacher waits until we're all in the listening position and then we sit in the listening position to do reflection. Reflection makes you calm and nice and if you don't sit nicely it won't make you calm and nice.

Chloe

The children have adapted this position to make it into a 'reflective position' with heads bent and hands facing downwards, which they adopt after the candle has been lit. Eyes are often closed; sometimes they are left open in order to focus on the candle flame.

Agreed rules

It is also important that rules are set and agreed at the beginning of the session. Once these have been agreed it is not usually necessary to continue this discussion. The rules usually include such ones as no quick

When the candle's on you have music on so that you can think inside your head.

Chloe

movement, unnecessary toilet visits or shouting out. These rules are important in terms of health and safety as much as spirituality. It is extremely important that these rules are agreed with the children and adhered to. The time of day is often important in the success of reflection time, as there are 'critical times' when experience alerts you to the fact that something negative is about to take place. This would not be the best time to enter into the reflection process, particularly in the early days.

Regular times

Although in my experience reflection time can work during the morning, it seems to feel more 'right' during the afternoon. It is an ideal project to initiate during the autumn term because as the afternoons draw in it is very satisfying to gather around the 'spiritual campfire'. It is also important to consider who is present at this time, as it can become a very special time in the day. It would seem relevant to consider preparing other adults who are likely to be present as it would indeed be unfortunate if someone were suddenly to get up and begin to wash the paint pots in the middle of what is potentially a significant spiritual experience. If the children are already used to circle time as being a special time the reflection time becomes quite an easy and related version of circle time.

Rituals

We already meet for a 'sharing' time when children sit in a circle and a special stone (we have two from Ireland, and one of Aboriginal design) is passed from child to child as they share views and objects which are of significant personal relevance to them. This format is also used for reflection time. The availability of a CD player and access to suitable music are important and necessary components of a reflection time. Children tend to develop their own favourites; a collection of music that we have found to be suitable is listed in Appendix 3. The classics are usually from native American or Tibetan chants and the theme music from the film *Titanic*. These pieces of music are also used for entrance music for assemblies or as background music to physical education sessions, which means that the children usually become quite familiar with them. The same music can also be used as the children come into the classroom at the beginning of the morning, which sets the scene for a calm atmosphere from the very beginning of the day. The candle is the central focus of reflection time and the reflection process. It is vital that it is talked about before the session begins. I have found that it is important to use a range of candles: large, fat, thin, perfumed and plain; the children tend to bring the candles in and so their ownership is again in evidence. We also have a large jug of water close at hand as a safety measure. It is also vital to discuss the 'reflection rules' so that the children are familiar with them. A strict routine is always observed and I suppose it almost becomes a ceremony:

1.   The door is closed.

2.   The lights are turned off.

3.   A jug of water is placed next to the candle. (The candles are always placed carefully on a plate.)

The children certainly enjoy the routines involved and have an understanding of the necessity of the routines. It would be a brave person who would dare to change these routines once they are in place. It must be remembered to insist that the children should not try this at home, although many of the children are used to their parents using candles and music at home to create atmosphere. It is important to insist that the children remain very still before the candle is lit. The music should already be playing in order to minimize movement or disruption; timing is usually dictated by the situation. If reflection time takes place at the end of the day it typically lasts for about 15 minutes. As new children are introduced to the situation they usually look around at other children for guidance and very quickly join in the simple routines and procedures.

Chapter 4

Reflection: the act

Model of reflection: setting it up

1. Allocate jobs such as being in charge of the jug of water, the notice on the door and switching off the lights.

2. Set up the room; place the candle in the middle of the carpet or communal area; gather together music, lighter, jug of water; place the notice on the door.

3. Discuss the process and the rules of reflection with the group:

    – sitting still is essential;

    – talking while the music is on is not allowed;

    – sharing of thoughts is optional;

    – there is a notice on the door to prevent disruption.

4. Go through the routine.

5. Make sure that everyone understands the importance of sitting still.

6. Put the jug of water next to the candle.

7. Turn the lights off.

8. Play the pre-selected music.

9. Light the candle.

10. Everyone should be quiet and the process can begin.

11. Blow out the candle.

12. Circle time takes place and the stone is passed around the group.

Reflection: the first time

CHILDREN

It is important that the children are sitting calmly in a circle around the candle before the session begins.

The most appropriate body language is discussed in Chapter 3; I have found that if all of the issues are discussed before the session, then everything runs a lot more smoothly than if it is necessary to stop to point out each little detail. Until the children become used to reflection time, there may be some attempts

Kevin

> The reason for reflection is you have to keep calm and not go around the room and walking around.

reflection

When we do reflection we sit in a listening position when Mrs White Lights the candle we Siting in a listening position and we look at the candle and don't take our ise off the candle we. have some music on too and we dont tok

at disruption. I have found that if these interruptions are ignored, then the rest of the children are able to concentrate; however, if the disruption is major then the whole process needs to be stopped so that this can be discussed. The fact that the candle is lit usually deters most children from moving, as they are either entranced or frightened that they will cause a fire. Perhaps this next comment contains some wishful thinking!

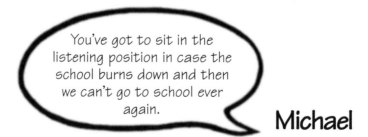

You've got to sit in the listening position in case the school burns down and then we can't go to school ever again.

Michael

It is useful actually to tell the children that they can close their eyes or look at the flame, but that they must not disturb anyone else by looking at them or distracting them. I have worked with children who have displayed very challenging behaviour, yet they have always remained calm during reflection time.

When Neil first came in he looked around the classroom and then he came to sit down and when we came to do reflection with him, he looked around at everyone and then he saw that everyone was sitting nicely and watching the candle, even when he was sitting scrappy, he never took his eyes off the candle. When everyone looks at the candle, people, when they are scrappy, people look at the candle while the music is on. They look at the candle and the music is all calm and nice and the candle is nice and so is the flame because it makes everyone calm because you get the flame which means that it is interesting.

Sally

It is relevant to mention at this point that the children in the project class felt that the whole classroom environment had a role to play in the success of reflection time.

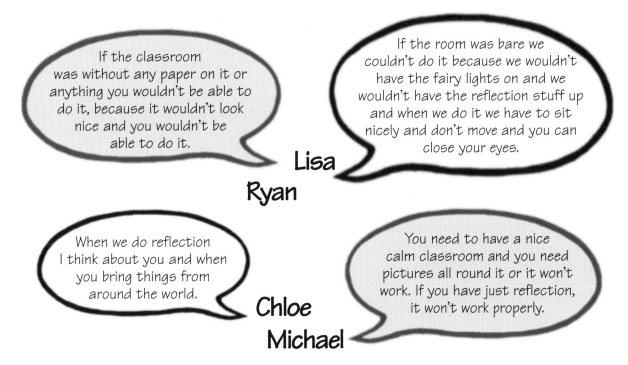

If the classroom was without any paper on it or anything you wouldn't be able to do it, because it wouldn't look nice and you wouldn't be able to do it.

Lisa

Ryan

If the room was bare we couldn't do it because we wouldn't have the fairy lights on and we wouldn't have the reflection stuff up and when we do it we have to sit nicely and don't move and you can close your eyes.

When we do reflection I think about you and when you bring things from around the world.

Chloe

Michael

You need to have a nice calm classroom and you need pictures all round it or it won't work. If you have just reflection, it won't work properly.

It is clear from these comments that the creation of a physical learning environment which is stimulating yet soft will help to support a reflective approach. If children help in the building of that environment then it is more likely to be successful. The attention paid to detail can pay dividends in the battle to deal with unacceptable behaviour. If children bring things to the room it helps them to feel part of the place; this is more important for some children than others, although they all enjoy contributing. This may only entail bringing a small important item to the classroom, although children do tend to become enthusiastic and if you are not careful you could have a classroom that resembles a flea market!

> When Neil came in, the candle was on and everyone was sitting nicely, Neil did that as well and the candle was all calm and so was the music and we all sat nicely in a listening position and we looked at the candle and all of the reflection stuff was nice and then sometimes when the candle's on, the flame's nice and all of the stuff around the classroom is calm and nice and because it's got like gold pictures and Buddhas and special mats and books and cloths and it's got two computers and pictures and the reflection cloth has got patterns on it and so has the candle.

Sally

The physical environment can have a dramatic effect on the behaviour of some children, so much so that they tend to cooperate because they don't want to leave the classroom. Although it is understandable to wish to send a child out of the room at times, research shows that it is important to keep this to a minimum, particularly for some children who need what Wills (1960) in McNamara and Moreton (1995, p. 29) calls 'safety, security and permanence'. As McNamara and Moreton have also found, in the case of children with emotional and behavioural difficulties 'the normal sanction of exclusion from the classroom needs to be at a minimum, questioned and (ideally) stopped'.

A final task is to discuss briefly what the word reflection means. When we have discussed it, it would appear that most children understand it simply as 'thinking back'. Having set the scene, as described in the previous chapter, and having created an appropriate and relevant atmosphere, the group should now be ready to enter into the process of reflection.

TIME OF DAY

There are a number of suitable times when reflection could be entered into for the first time. I have found it works best at the end of a wet or windy playtime or at the end of a hectic day. It is also an interesting way to begin a religious education lesson.

> When the candle's on I always think about Buddhas because I like the way they sit and they are nice and calm.

Kylie

I have also used reflection time as an introduction to a discussion about an important issue or before debating rules for classroom behaviour. It is also a useful tool to use at times when team building is in its early stages or when it is necessary to develop a specific class identity. Choosing the time of day is a crucial factor in ensuring the success of reflection time. For a group who is at the very beginning of an exploration of the benefits of reflection, the end of the day is probably the best place to start. Children are usually more receptive to this type of communal experience at this point in the day. They are often tired and quite used to 'receiving' a story at this time and are consequently more amenable to sitting and listening.

Do not disturb

Guaranteeing, as far as possible, that there are no interruptions to your reflection time is essential. It is important that the group is not disturbed or distracted as this could lead to a devaluation of the whole experience. It is also important that the room is made as dark as possible, perhaps closing blinds or drawing the curtains to windows or

> When you have reflection you need to look at the candle when you can't move or the school will set on fire and you have to have good body language and you close the door and put the sign on.

Lisa

to the quiet area. The door needs to be firmly closed and if this is not possible any piece of available furniture pulled across will indicate a need for privacy. There will always be problems with this situation: for example, my classroom has a door but no curtains; it is also situated underneath a particularly noisy classroom. However, it is important to try and make the best of any given situation.

Resources

Music

It is essential to pre-select any music that is required and to have it ready to use, as any last-minute searching would surely destroy the atmosphere, not to mention the safety aspects of such a situation. Any calm and quiet music would be suitable for an initial experience, although a group will usually choose and iden-tify any favourites. Different types of music work for differ-ent groups. It is relevant to allow children to listen to a wide range of music in order to develop their critical skills. This is also a way into other areas of learning which are described in further detail in Chapter 8. A collection of music titles that I have found to be suitable for use with younger children is available in Appendix 3, although I find that I am constantly reviewing this list. A firm favourite with

one group of children is not always the choice of another group. If children are involved in the choice of music it also enables them to have more ownership of the whole experience. You will find that they have quite strong views and preferences about what they think will work: we now have quite a collection on our shelf. You will also find that as the children become more involved they will want to bring in their own candles and other bits and pieces!

CANDLES

In my experience a large candle is more effective for reflection time. In our classroom the candle is usually placed on a plate, which is then placed on another object, which raises it higher than eye level. I use an upturned plastic box covered with a patterned cloth, which is placed on our 'special' rug. This collection of reflection equipment remains on the carpet most of the time and incredibly it remains untouched. This is quite remarkable as the class has a membership of 30 and many of the children are extremely boisterous. I think that it also indicates that there is something special going on here and that the reflection materials are part of it, therefore they are treated with respect.

LIGHTER

It is useful to have a lighter close by and of course it must be kept out of the way of small fingers!

A JUG OF WATER

In my classroom a child has responsibility for placing the jug of water next to the candle. It means that this vital safety measure is never forgotten.

Timing

The time it takes to conduct a reflection time varies; it may take about 10 minutes or longer, although to begin with it is probably advisable to keep it short, extending it as the group becomes more used to it. The ending of a piece of music usually indicates a natural finishing point. It may be useful to make your own tape containing sections of music and in this way you are more in control of the timing. We have a system where one child each day is appointed as the 'child of the day', which means that this child is picked for all of the 'special jobs' during the day, and this child is also picked to blow out the candle at the end of reflection time. Sometimes a child who usually finds it difficult to remain calm for an extended time and has made a special effort to do so during reflection time may be chosen for this task, thus adding an extra incentive for cooperative behaviour. Blowing out candles is a much-loved activity! It is extremely difficult to be prescriptive about the amount of time reflection time takes, as it is often dependent on the purpose of the session or the dynamics of the participating group.

Afterwards

After the session, children may choose to discuss the activity or what they were thinking about or they may choose to keep their thoughts private. Respecting this choice is all part of the process. The children often enjoy the power of being able to say, 'My thoughts are private'. The stone is passed around the circle and only the child holding the stone may speak. As you can see from these comments the children tend to think about a wide range of subjects.

I like when the candle's on because you can think about anything and you can think about different countries and the people who haven't got any toys. I'm looking for things I can give away to other people who haven't got any toys. Sometimes when the candle's on I think about my mum and my teacher.

Chloe

When you do reflection you've got a picture in your head you have to colour and you've forgot what to do, when you do reflection again you can think of that picture again.

Kevin

I like reflection because you can close your eyes and I always get a picture of when we are doing the cats dance.

Sally

When the candle's on I keep thinking about Jesus and how he died.

David

At reflection I thought about when I was playing on my computer and won every single bit and I didn't want to do it all over again so I switched the computer off.

Greg

I thought of my hamster when it bit me and it bit my sister and then my dad said he was going to get rid of it if the hamster still bites.

Tim

Chapter 5

A wider educational context

If reflection time is used at the end of the school day it is possible to create a calm communal atmosphere in which to end what is usually a hectic and pressurized day. However, a reflection time could be adapted to introduce a religious education lesson, when it would possibly create a more spiritual atmosphere appropriate to the lesson which is about to take place. At the present time in education, there is so much emphasis placed on how to teach children that it is quite refreshing to be able to focus on how children learn. Reflection time is a tool to open up how children learn and to allow adults to learn alongside children, moving away from the role of instructor for a while. I believe that the use of reflection in this way has improved the learning that takes place in my classroom; it has also had a significant impact on behaviour. These are issues that are discussed in greater detail later in the book. I have listened to children talking about the effect of reflection time; I have recorded and transcribed their views as part of my research project and I have been moved by some of their comments. These children often struggle to find language to express their feelings, which can lead to personal frustration and low levels of academic achievement. I believe that reflection time has given these children time to think and to formulate views before trying to express them.

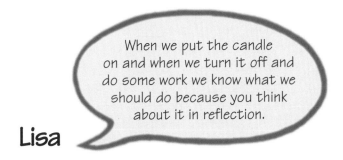

When we put the candle on and when we turn it off and do some work we know what we should do because you think about it in reflection.

Lisa

Reflection time allows the children the time to become calm and to share, without the pressure that sometimes exists at other times in the school day. They don't have to perform or to speak if they don't want to.

You look at the candle and you see yourself.

Shauna

It gives you peace.

Callum

It is obvious from these comments that reflection time is a meaningful process for the children. It is a way of being able to make a fresh start, especially for those who have been in trouble in some way during the day.

Trust and responsibility

In the everyday classroom situation a tool such as reflection time enables the teacher to find out what is going on for many of the children in the class. It moves away from the pressure that is often present in terms of teaching a syllabus with all its associated planning and assessment procedures. It moves the work into the area of a child's 'other' development. It takes education into the areas of social, moral, cultural and spiritual development. This particular area has always been so difficult to assess; yet focusing on this important area can lay strong foundations for a child's personal development and consequent attitudes to lifelong learning and relationships. It is a powerful tool allowing valuable interaction between adults and children that might not otherwise take place. Reflection time involves a process that must be handled with care and sensitivity if the learning experiences are to be positive and memorable. There is a definite need for time in which all children are able to clarify their thoughts and this is certainly the case for those who are struggling with language and have difficulty expressing themselves. It is a way to help children to develop the confidence to express themselves in a safe and comfortable environment. Although teaching is in part about instruction, this type of environment encourages an approach to teaching which combines instruction with a freedom to express oneself as an independent individual. The reflective approach also involves the teacher sharing in that learning process. It means that an atmosphere of trust, respect and support must exist. Although empowering the child to speak as an autonomous individual is a priority, it is also important to create opportunities for this development to take place in a structured way so that the maximum learning can take place. The music, the candle and the timing of reflection time all bring a structured environment, which supports the learning of young children as they move into the world of deeper self-expression. It is so important to value all contributions and to value privacy at all times. Reflection time also has the potential to be an intimate and a spiritual occasion. In order for this to be the case a genuine commitment to the process of reflection needs to exist. The teacher is allowed a rare glimpse into the world of the child and consequently is able to learn about learning. In the beginning such a process may appear to be challenging and even slightly daunting and it does take time to develop the necessary trust and confidence to feel that reflection time is also a successful time. However, I have found that it is worthwhile and that there are many rewards for such a commitment to this type of classroom development. If treated with respect and sincerity, the reflection process can lead to a discussion of feelings that may never surface at any other time of the day.

Chapter 6

Issues

The role of the school

Teaching children how to respond to situations within an environment which is open and where children feel able to talk about just about anything is surely as much a responsibility of the school as ensuring high standards in literacy and numeracy.

Evidence such as that provided by the Elton Report (1989) has proved that there are established links between learning and behaviour, which leads to the belief that the promotion and guarantee of positive calm behaviour can only lead to the raising of academic standards. Although it is important to explore the potential for children supporting each other through a mentoring system, for example, it is also important not to forget the crucial role of the teacher as model. As teachers we need to consider reflecting on our own behaviour in order to identify areas for change. Teaching is certainly difficult and sometimes we are not as patient and wonderful as we would like to be. However, if we do display impatience and verbal aggression it offers an opportunity to discuss why we may have behaved in such a way and what the best response would have been. It takes courage to admit to mistakes in behaviour but it is an extremely effective way to get a point across. I feel that we expect children to behave in ways that we as adults cannot achieve. For example, it has always amused me that we expect children to be quiet at the end of an assembly. A successful assembly may have been provocative and interactive, yet when it is over we expect the children immediately to become calm and controlled. How different from the adult behaviour exhibited at the end of a film, concert or play when everyone wants to discuss what has just been witnessed and experienced. It would surely make more sense to allow children to react to what has just happened before requiring a calmer atmosphere in order to leave the hall or room safely. The ability to consider situations from a child's point of view can be a supportive teaching tool. Sometimes it can be the case where the culture of the school or the area promotes a belief that if shouting occurs it means that something has been sorted out. On a number of occasions in the past I have witnessed parents who prefer a teacher who shouts because 'she knows how to sort them out'. Consider the view that if the children were really 'sorted out' the teacher wouldn't have to shout so much. McNamara and Moreton (1995, pp. 33–4) agree that, although at times shouting through frustration is understandable, there can be a very powerful backlash as a result of verbal aggression: 'Teachers who gain and hold on to classroom power through verbal aggression are likely, through modelling that behaviour, to have it turned on them by some pupils.' As teachers we often complain about children shouting, yet it may be that this occurs partly as a result of our own behaviour. The authors also discovered that children have learnt this lesson in power assertion from the adults and teachers in their previous experience. Children certainly don't like being shouted at:

Children have told me how upset they are by shouting and how much they value being spoken to with respect within a calm environment. This respectful approach, according to children, helps them to change their own behaviour. Therefore, teacher attitude and style can have a resounding effect on changing unacceptable behaviour.

New children

If new children join the class during the year, they tend to follow the routines and behaviours of the more established children. In my experience the new children tend to quickly form a commitment to the reflection process. The existing class members tend to take responsibility when it comes to explaining why and how things are done.

I recently found myself in a situation where I had to entertain a class at very short notice, at the end of a very hectic day. This is not unusual in a primary school; however, instead of reading the usual story to a large number of children, I decided to try out reflection time. This involved a group of 60 children ranging from five years old to seven years old from two separate classes, and included 2 children from a completely different class. This was a very large group for a reflection time by anybody's standards. I was amazed that all of the children who were present immediately became involved in the session, adopting the correct body language, some closing eyes, others focusing on the flame. As the stone was passed around at the end of the session the children talked animatedly about what they had been thinking about and what they had just experienced. As time goes by and the reflection process becomes part of the classroom routine, other children from different classes seem to be drawn into it. There is a feeling that 'something special' is going on. This has implications for staff in other classes; not all staff will be convinced of the benefits of using such an approach or will feel confident enough to try out this method. I firmly believe that it must be personal choice for teachers; however, if the benefits of such an approach are visible, such as the changes in behaviour of identified children who are known to be difficult, then interest is often stirred. A personal commitment to the approach is a necessary condition for its success, therefore any half-hearted attempts, which are management driven, are likely to fail.

Gender

During the course of my work in this particular school, many of the major difficulties we have experienced in terms of behaviour have involved boys who have displayed disruptive and violent behaviour. As McNamara and Moreton (1995, p. 83) discovered, some boys display different types of learning needs and may need extra skills training. An awareness of this helps in terms of analysing what is going on in the area of behaviour both within the classroom and outside in the playground. The Reflection Project has focused on helping boys to express their feelings in less aggressive ways through discussion, mentoring and dance.

Chapter 7

Special educational needs

Reflection and special needs

With respect to special educational needs it is important to focus on a definition of what this term means within the context of this particular project and book. It is generally accepted that children with special educational needs will be experiencing learning, emotional and behavioural difficulties, or have physical needs due to disability. However, an individual child's needs may belong to one or more of these categories and in some cases to all of them at the same time. There is sometimes confusion about the definition of emotional and behavioural difficulties and whether a child with emotional and behavioural difficulties has special needs. Any teacher who has worked with children with emotional and behavioural difficulties will probably agree that these children do indeed have special needs. Within the context of this work I have also referred to some children as having special needs because they were underachieving due to difficulties with language. Some of the children in the project class were emotionally distressed due to dealing with the death of a parent, the birth of a sibling, responsibility and grief. Some children were displaying challenging and disruptive behaviour, which meant that the everyday work of the classroom could not proceed as smoothly as it should have done. There were children in the group who found concentrating on a task difficult to maintain and there were children who were enthusiastic about school but had difficulties understanding the requirements of the National Curriculum. Therefore for the purposes of this work special needs became an issue because learning, emotional and behavioural difficulties combined to form a barrier to achievement.

Reflection and behaviour modification

In the project school many children found it difficult to function as part of either a small or large group. Some of the children found it difficult to sit still, to listen for extended periods of time, to focus and to think. The school, as many schools do, also experienced difficulties coping with children's behaviour at lunchtimes. In my classroom, reflection time not only provided time for children to think but it also had a positive effect on the behaviour of some of the children at lunchtimes.

When Trevor first arrived at the project school, he was sent off the playground almost every lunchtime because he punched and kicked other children. When questioned about the reasons for this violence, Trevor claimed that other children were 'winding him up' and calling him names. Trevor found that reflection time gave him some of the skills he needed to deal with this situation, although it was also the responsibility of the school to investigate the allegations that Trevor made about other children and to prevent such situations from occurring. Trevor's behaviour changed so much that he was never sent inside at lunchtime and eventually he became a mentor to a younger child.

> Well at dinnertime I never get sent to the red bench because all I do is reflection with David and after dinner sometimes we do it at the morning play and sometimes the teachers say that we've been good and David. When we go in the yard we'll take our shoes off and we sit in a listening position and we close our eyes and when people talk to us we just we just don't listen to them we ignore them and just keep on doing reflection. In the yard some of my friends I do reflection and some of my friends they start doing it with me and that's when I ask my best friend if he'll do it with me and his name is David and he's the same age as me and when some people talk to me and Ian we just ignore them because we're meditating.

Trevor

Reflection time can enable certain children to become calm at 'risk' times when they could experience difficulty in cooperating and responding to requests or directions.

It can provide an answer to the 'fallout' from wet and windy playtimes and lunchtimes and any strategy that cuts down the amount of time spent sorting out difficult situations actually raises standards of achievement for all concerned as it allows more time to be spent on the education process. It is often the case that the majority of children who behave in a positive manner lose valuable learning time due to the negative behaviour of the minority.

> When I first got into school I was a bit scrappy and now I've decided to do reflection at playtime it's stopped me from getting into trouble and at dinner times I do it and then I start playing with the hoops and then people and then I go back to do reflection and people keep on talking to me and I don't listen to them I just keep on sitting in a listening position.

Trevor

Case studies

There are five case studies in this section. Three of the children were in phase 1 of the research project and two of the children were in phase 2.

1. PROFILE OF TREVOR, AGED SEVEN (PHASE 1)

Trevor had attended a number of different schools before joining the project school. He lived with his two young brothers and his mother. Trevor tended to assume a great deal of responsibility for his younger brothers and he also appeared to be very protective towards his mother:

> 66 My name's Trevor and I am seven years old and my mum's had a new baby and it's two days old and when I went to visit her I cheered her up by giving her a big hug. 99

Trevor was a sensitive, mature child who also displayed challenging and violent behaviour, particularly at breaktimes and lunchtimes. He found it difficult to settle into school and complained of racist name-calling and bullying, although he said that most of this took place outside of the school situation.

> 66 At reflection time I was thinking about other people's colour skin and bullies and how they dress and what colour they are. Sometimes when other people are different colours than white, some people will call them racist names and em we've got a Buddha in this classroom and I always look at it and think about what do Buddhas look like. 99

However, Trevor's behaviour changed significantly during his time in the project class and he began enthusiastically to use the skills he was learning during reflection time to modify his own negative behaviour. He talks about reflection 'clearing all of the bad things out of his head' and goes on to explain:

> 66 The bad things in my head is when I fight and when I am loud in the classroom sometimes I get told off and then my teacher tells us to be sensible. 99

Trevor's self-esteem increased and his behaviour changed so much that he became a role model for other children in the class, taking the role of mentor to a younger boy in the group. He also helped other children to understand what was happening for them:

> 66 When James's going to assembly like when he's sitting down it might just go out of his head that he's got to be good and that's when he changes to be naughty. 99

At times, Trevor told me that he found life at home difficult and it would appear from his comments on tape that reflection helped him to deal with the pressures of both his school and domestic situations. Trevor used the reflection techniques at home (without a candle) to help him to think.

> **❝** I think reflection is good because it clears all the bad things out of your head and the only time I can do it is if my brothers are asleep and my mum is watching television downstairs that is the only way I can do it. **❞**

Reflection took on a deep significance for Trevor at this particular point in his life and I feel that it offered him a strategy, however small, for coping with difficult situations. Many of the children talk about reflection as a cleansing time, when they are able to remove bad things and embark on a fresh start:

> **❝** Well reflection means you come to the best part of your life because that's the only thing that clears out your head. **❞**

2. Profile of James, aged seven (phase 1)

James's academic and social development had been the cause for concern since he had joined the school's nursery unit at the age of three. James would regularly have violent tantrums and he liked to lock himself in toilets. As he got older he claimed that he could hear voices in his head and, as he became able to talk about what was happening to him, James claimed that it was the voices in his head that made him do bad things. James's academic progress was very restricted and at the end of Year 2 he was just about able to write his own name. He always made a huge fuss at the beginning of every day, screaming and crying and refusing to enter the classroom and he was also violent towards adults and other children, needing constant one-to-one support when he was in school. Although James did have the support of a nursery nurse every day we tended to keep him within the classroom so that he was able to form and sustain some relationships with his peers and so that he would feel a part of our team. It appeared, from my observations and from James's comments, that reflection provided something of a therapeutic outlet for his pain and anger. He visibly physically relaxed during these sessions. James's learning support assistant and I worked closely together to try to develop ways to deal with this situation. We found that our priorities were to find ways to deal with James's behaviour and to prevent other children from becoming hurt and distressed. We felt that we needed to limit the amount of time we were spending just concentrating on this one child instead of teaching the rest of the class and addressing their learning and emotional needs. James's behaviour was upsetting to witness both for myself, James's learning support assistant and other children in the class. We adopted two approaches to deal with this very serious situation: one was the long-term development of a reflection time and another was a short-term approach which involved the use of a sheet of paper to record critical incidents. The paper had a line drawn down the middle of it and it had the word 'good' on the top of one column and the word 'bad' on the top of the other column. James chose these terms, as he always talked about his 'good side' and his 'bad side'. The use of this paper after particularly violent episodes seemed to calm James when negotiation and reasoning failed. It was as if he could remove the blame for his actions from himself and attribute the negative behaviour to his 'bad side'. There seemed to be a constant battle raging inside James and at times we felt helpless to know what to do. James struggled so much to find the language to express himself and often as a result of his inability to communicate effectively he ended up in a frustrated and violent rage. James regularly pushed everyone away from him, throwing objects and eventually crumpling into a sobbing heap. We desperately wanted to help James and at times we found ourselves acting instinctively in the haste to find ways to support him. I did not feel qualified to deal with the extremity of this particular situation. I know that teachers, nursery nurses and classroom assistants often find themselves coping with similar situations whilst doubting their effectiveness to do so. This is James describing himself and some of his lunchtime behaviour:

> 66 My name James Michael and I'm seven old and now run about on playground, for us dinner time I was on the bench and up to juniors and then I do some paper like bad side and good side why you picked me? I thought I was going to assembly because I don't like assembly. 99

He knows that he was on the red bench (a PE bench at the side of the school hall where children sit when they have been removed from the playground at lunchtime) as a direct result of his negative behaviour. James's language development is obviously restricted, yet he is able to get across the feeling that there are forces inside his head that are working against each other and that they are responsible for his unacceptable behaviour:

> 66 Cos my brain keeps putting it in and I pulled it out when it stayed in for long. Got the bad one out now I got to get the good one out cos cos my good one is naughty and the bad one is good and I keep saying no you're not. I got two of them right and they keep going back in again at school and I keep saying no. I like school but it keep saying don't like school. 99

Reflection time allowed James some peace and calm in an otherwise potentially violent and turbulent day:

> 66 Reflection's about when you look at the candle on and we be quiet. When sometimes I won't sit down I cos I keep getting out when it reflection many will go out of my head I think so. 99

3. PROFILE OF JOSEPH, AGED SEVEN (PHASE 1)

Joseph was a very quiet and hard-working member of the class; however, during the course of the project, Joseph's father died and he was present in the house when this took place. This had an obvious effect on his behaviour and emotional development, and he became withdrawn and, at times, reluctant to work. The only time he ever talked about how he felt about his loss was at reflection time.

> 66 My name's Joseph and I like reflection because you can think about somebody you really like and you've lost and you can't have them because they was really special and now you only can see them in the grave. 99

Reflection time enabled Joseph to think about what had happened to him and it also gave him a secure environment in which to discuss his feelings. It also allowed me to gain some insight into how he was feeling, which I otherwise might have missed during a busy day. Joseph eventually became more communicative and regained his positive approach to classroom work.

4. PROFILE OF RYAN, AGED 7 (PHASE 2)

Ryan was a capable child with a very supportive family background. However, he found sitting still for any length of time, listening, and focusing on any task extremely difficult to achieve. Ryan was often in trouble as a result of the way in which he spoke to adults and at times he was less than supportive towards younger and less able children. Ryan responded extremely well to a reflective approach, so much so that he became a mentor to a younger child from another class who eventually moved to our class. Ryan enjoyed reflection time: it helped him to become calm and to gain some physical self-control, which in turn helped him to settle down to work and consequently raised his academic achievement. Ryan achieved above average results in the Standard Assessment Tests during the summer term 1999.

> ❝ I like reflection because it helps you to think about how your behaviour's going to be. When you're looking at the candle you can think what you want and if you can't do work you can think about it when you're looking at the candle. ❞

Gradually, during the project year, Ryan became calm enough to cope with his own work and cooperated to the point where he was able to become a role model for a younger child who was also finding classroom life difficult to cope with. Neil was a six-year-old child from another class who gradually joined our class for reflection and dance sessions before becoming a more permanent member of the class towards the end of the Reflection Project. It was Ryan's task to collect Neil from his classroom, which was located at the other end of the school.

> ❝ A mentor means to me that I tell people what to do at reflection and then if I tell them they might do it and it changes their body language. I done it for Neil because he used to be all scrappy and I feel good now because I like doing stuff for people. When I bring him from his classroom because he always runs through the hall and I say stop and sometimes I have to say walk and then sometimes he doesn't do it. He copies me when I tell him to do reflection properly. ❞

Neil always sat next to Ryan during reflection times and copied his body language:

> ❝ When Neil does reflection he thinks about, he tells me at playtime, he thinks about his family. ❞

The development of the relationship between the two boys helped Ryan to appreciate the negative effects of his own behaviour on others:

> ❝ When Neil first came into the classroom he used to be scrappy and then he used to go under tables and in his classroom, but when I took him down to our class, he was nice and calm. ❞

Ryan became very involved in the dance project and because the other boys perceived him to be a leader, they too became enthusiastic:

> 66 Dance makes Neil good because when he dances Carl [Neil's dance mentor] tells him what to do and then he does it and then Simon sometimes dances and Neil starts to copy. When you go to discos and something and girls say that boys don't dance but when you go to school and do something like Cats and you watch a video before it and if you try it and you'll be able to feel like you are proud and all the boys will do it. 99

4. PROFILE OF NEIL, AGED SIX (PHASE 2)

At the beginning of the research project, Neil was in a different class from the project class and it was obvious that he was experiencing many difficulties. For example, he was unco-operative, disruptive and very successful in finding as many ways as he could to gain attention. In response to this situation Neil was spending increasing amounts of time in the project classroom and during this time we would often have reflection time. Gradually, the project class decided that Ryan would become Neil's mentor. It was Ryan's job to go to Neil's class to collect him every time we had reflection. Another child, Carl, a close friend of Ryan's, also became Neil's dance mentor. This relationship worked well for both Neil and Carl, because Carl, who lacked in self-confidence as a result of severe speech problems, also gained in self-esteem as a result of the dance project and his mentoring role. Carl collected Neil from his classroom and brought him to the hall for dance sessions. This relationship had a positive effect on Carl's development and he not only gained in confidence but he also became less aggressive towards others. Carl:

> 66 I like dancing and it makes me happy and I always dance. Dance is my best thing. 99

Neil responded well to the reflection time, the dance project and mentoring scheme and towards the end of the project year it was decided that Neil should join the class on a permanent basis. However, it is still early days and although Neil's behaviour has improved as a result of a reflective approach he still needs a carefully designed and structured individual programme to guide him through each day.

I believe that reflection time has enabled the children in the project class to have quality time to think and to talk. It has raised their self-esteem, which in turn has raised their academic performance.

PART TWO

Broad
School Issues

Chapter 8

Links with curriculum areas

I Like reflection because
I think of Lts of things
and its Nice and calm But we
put The candle on with a
Lighter and It makes Yuo
feeL good and I Sometimes
think I want to have a pet.

Language development and the requirements of the National Curriculum

Language development is not only the key to success in all areas of the curriculum, it is also important in terms of holistic child development as there is also the language of emotion and feeling which needs to be taught and developed. The importance of speaking and listening as mechanisms linking all National Curriculum subjects has already been mentioned earlier in this book; however, speaking and listening skills specifically play a strategic role in terms of meeting the requirements of the National Literacy Strategy. The introduction of the National Literacy

Strategy has had a huge impact on classroom practice. The time it takes to plan and to deliver a literacy hour has affected development in other areas and at the time of writing we are embarking on the Numeracy Strategy. These drives to raise standards in the core subjects are well intentioned and a great deal of money and time has gone into their development. The reality is of course that these initiatives are all well and good when working in certain circumstances. Certain conditions need to exist in the classroom if the literacy and numeracy strategies are to be effective. Consider what happens if a class of children, who are being presented with the literacy and numeracy strategies, are unable to listen effectively and to contribute to the shared sessions. What happens if they are unable to cooperate, and to function independently in their group activities, whilst the teacher concentrates on one particular group. What happens in the classroom where a child uses the opportunity, when the teacher is focused on one group, to terrorize other children with violent threats and abusive body language. A reflective approach contributes to the provision of a suitable learning environment for the delivery of the literacy and numeracy strategies. The development of such an environment is continuous and although there can be 'good times' when all appears to be running smoothly, it is part of a process which needs constant attention and adjustment. The development of an effective learning approach through which the National Curriculum and religious education can be delivered is a priority, but the spiritual growth of children also needs to be considered. It is important, as Hay and Nye (1998, p. 174) say, to maintain a balance between the legitimate requirements of an education system on the one hand and attention to the spiritual growth of children within it.

Religious education

There is a danger as a result of a certain and distanced approach to the teaching of religious education that religions are actually being represented and presented as separate from people's lives and lifestyles. As I have explored different ways of teaching religious education, it has become clear to me that issues of race and gender also need to be discussed. This can be daunting, as race and gender issues belong to an area that can be difficult to be embrace. It would be so easy to avoid the issues and just teach the bare facts about religions; however, if we are to prepare children for life in society it is important to help them to develop the thinking skills to tackle some of the important questions in life. It is also important to let children know that we as adults do not have all of the answers to these questions and that we can explore some of the issues together. I have found that, just like children, religions do not come in neat packages. Although religious education can be a difficult subject to teach it can also be a most fascinating subject for both children and adults. Children tend to be intrigued by the characters from the different religions and are attracted to the exploration of artefacts. The effective teaching of religious education is certainly a means to 'open up the world' to children who might otherwise have a more restricted view.

Citizenship

It would appear that citizenship is set to become high on the educational agenda and to become a statutory part of the school timetable in the revised curriculum. Day et al. (1998, p. 204) talk about the hallmarks of citizenship as being: 'Obeying school rules, developing the ability to control impulsiveness, turn-taking, working collaboratively for the collective good, becoming a group member, looking out for others, managing difference and diversity'. This definition has implications for the teaching of moral and social responsibility to very young children. It is anticipated that the citizenship curriculum will come into force in the year 2001 for Key Stage 1 children and 2002 for Key Stage 2 children. A reflective approach as described in this book provides a suitable platform for exploration of the issues as presented by a citizenship curriculum. The issues emerging are those of expression of personal opinion; reflection on issues of social and moral concern and participation in debate. In my own practice I have found that reflection time has helped to give children valuable time to think and when they did actually make a verbal contribution to a session it was usually pertinent because they had had time to think about what they were going to say. Although this particular tool can be used as an aid to teaching religious education and as a pathway to social, moral, spiritual and cultural development, it is also a relevant approach to teaching other subjects. As a general approach, the reflective approach has proved itself to be a proactive way to enable children to become more involved in the wider education process.

Justice

How many times do we hear the cry 'It's not fair!' and how many times do we pay attention to this? The feelings that accompany injustice can often build up and turn into aggression at a later stage. If time is taken to analyse a specific incident, it often turns out that the cause of the problem lies in the aftermath of something that has happened in the past. If situations are not dealt with quickly and effectively, then they often turn into deeper conflicts, which can take even longer to disentangle. An open ethos where children feel able to voice their concerns and know that they will be dealt with fairly can minimize disruption and the time-wasting that is often caused by protracted investigations into alleged causes of conflict.

Spiritual and moral development

Teachers are expected to focus on the spiritual and moral development of the children in their care. Whilst it is possible to assess children's achievement in maths, for instance through a Standard Assessment Task, it is not so easy or desirable to make such assessments in the area of spiritual and moral development. The use of a reflection time to provide a suitable learning environment in which spiritual and moral development can take place enables the teacher to find out about a child's development in these areas.

Multicultural education and anti-racist teaching

The anti-racist agenda of the 1970s and 1980s appeared to have been pushed aside with the advent of the National Curriculum. However, it reappears at certain times, for example during the inquiry into the death of Stephen Lawrence. Multicultural education should be about more than just learning facts and acquiring knowledge, it enters the realms of anti-racist teaching when it is centred on the exploration of attitudes and values. A time needs to be created in schools when such attitudes can be explored within a secure framework. The reflective approach is also about challenging stereotypes and providing positive and realistic images and information about all of the groups in society. There are obvious links between social, spiritual, moral and cultural development and religious education, but religious education should also be about the positive representation and interpretation of ethnic and cultural diversity within a pluralist society. Although anti-racism, multicultural education and religious education are inextricably linked, since the 1980s anti-racists have condemned a multicultural approach as being too focused on the exotic and the superficial. As Jackson (1997, p. 74) says, anti-racists complained that such superficiality reinforced platitudes and stereotypes and helped racism to remain intact. He agrees that the teaching of religious education is fraught with dangers in terms of cultural assumptions contained in some of its teaching materials and sometimes in its delivery in the classroom. However, Jackson (1997, p. 76) reassures that an important element of teaching religious education is 'to look for more flexible ways of representing and interpreting cultural material which take on board key elements of the anti-racist critique'. Reflection time is often the time when children share some of their views on society, and it can therefore provide the starting point for development in this area. There were common views within the project group, for instance, that all people with brown skin would speak a language other than English. In the past I have worked on projects with Key Stage 1 children which have attempted to address anti-racist issues. An example of my work, 'The Red and Green Story', which may help with starting points in this area, is contained in Appendix 4.

Chapter 9

Staff development issues

Case study

Two teachers with a job-share arrangement taught one of the Year 1 classes in the project school. During the project year both teachers found that they were experiencing difficulties as a result of the behaviour of a small group of boys in the class. The boys were failing to cooperate with the teachers and they were also disrupting the education of the majority of the pupils in the class. One boy in particular, Neil, was becoming more and more out of control. Neil's behaviour is discussed in greater detail in the case study section of Chapter 7.

Action

As part of the school's group appraisal scheme, the staff had agreed to focus on the areas of planning and behaviour management. The scheme was entitled: 'Planning for Better Behaviour' and was due to start at the beginning of the autumn term following the project year. However, part of the scheme began during the summer term 1999 for the job-share teachers. In response to the teachers' request for support, a framework was used to identify their needs, to structure development and to provide a record of the development experience. In my role as staff development coordinator I carried out an observation of Neil in the classroom situation and in the hall during a physical education session. The framework for the observation was agreed with the teacher beforehand and the results of the observation were discussed with both of the teachers the day after it was carried out. Each teacher was given a copy of the observation results and together we discussed the list of possible strategies that could be used to improve the situation. These strategies were quite broad by necessity as it is well known that what works for one teacher does not necessarily work for another. The important element of this exercise was to offer support and choices to the staff concerned. It is essential to listen to staff and to record their concerns in order to work out a way forward. Neil was also involved in this process and his views were added to the development document.

Whole school development

Issues

The reflective approach to teaching and learning is based on the belief that a child is part of the whole school. A child may be in a particular classroom for most of each day, but the care of the child is the responsibility of all of the adult workers in the school. Children move around school and between classes; they attend assemblies and play outside and it is during these times that they may be receiving mixed messages from the adults with whom they are interacting. However, if a management programme of development and training for staff is to be effective it should have a commitment to whole school issues at its centre. The use of a professional development structure is one mechanism which can be used to ensure whole school development. However, a culture of openness for staff and pupils needs to exist in order for any of these schemes to be successful. Good training can lead to empowerment and the raising of self-esteem, but mechanisms need to be in place to support staff who may feel under pressure to manage their own stress and may even feel bullied and threatened.

INTERNAL AND EXTERNAL TRAINING

Although it may be possible to provide good quality 'in-house' staff development programmes based on first-hand knowledge of a school and its community, it is important to strike a balance between internal and external provision. Outside facilitation often brings a fresh view of a school's situation, particularly in terms of behaviour management issues. It is also important for all staff to be able to leave the building for training purposes because when staff attend training at other venues it allows for the important facility of networking to take place.

THE ROLE OF LEARNING SUPPORT ASSISTANTS/NURSERY NURSES

Many of the classroom workers carrying out the role of special needs or learning support assistant find themselves dealing with situations for which they have neither been prepared nor trained. The issue of training is an important one for schools as some external courses may not be relevant to the needs of an individual school. Budget restrictions can also mean that nursery nurses and learning support assistants are at the end of a long queue when it comes to professional development. Training need not be expensive or unattainable. It is possible to provide in-house training through the sharing of case studies and strategies that have been developed as a result of practice within the school. Families or groups of schools can also provide training systems and support networks for their workers. The point is that acknowledgement and identification of the training needs of support workers is a priority in the development of whole school approaches. The inclusion of special needs nursery nurses and learning support assistants in meetings and the decision-making process is vital to the success of a team approach, particularly in the application of individual education plans for children with special educational needs. A child with special needs is still part of a class, a school and an education system and although a child may have been allocated time with an assistant, it is important to decide on the most appropriate way to use this time in each individual case.

INVOLVEMENT OF PARENTS AND FAMILIES

There is already statutory involvement of parents through the Special Needs Code of Practice. It is the quality of these relationships that is important, as the communication of information needs to be sensitively handled. Parents in partnership as a concept is important to the whole school situation, but in terms of special educational needs it takes on an even greater significance. I have always felt that the family role should also be of significance as I feel that sometimes the role of the wider family is not taken into consideration. As Day et al. (1998, p. 201) have found, children whose behaviour may be perceived as challenging and who may risk school exclusion particularly need their families and teachers to work in close collaboration. This is a view also supported by Webster-Stratton and Herbert (1995) in Day et al. (1998): 'To enhance the success of school-based interventions with pupils who demonstrate challenging behaviour, it is vital that families work together with teachers to ensure a consistency of approach to raising standards of social interaction, learning to control impulsivity and developing self-awareness.'

LINKS WITH NEXT PHASE OF EDUCATION

A school's development can be affected by its physical and age group arrangements and there are particular issues affecting separate infant and junior schools as opposed to primary schools. Moreover, some schools, as in the case of the project school, may also have nursery units. The project school nursery staff played a vital role in the early identification of, and support for, children with special educational needs. There will always be inherent difficulties with communication between infant and junior schools by the very nature of the arrangement. Communication between schools may be dependent upon similarities and differences between vision and ethos of the two schools; attitude of the head teachers; staff relationships; and historical and cultural factors. In the case of the Reflection Project it was difficult to monitor the progress of the children after they left the project school because they moved to a separate school situation.

CORPORATE RESPONSIBILITY

It is the responsibility of both school and parents in partnership to ensure the best possible education for each child. Unfortunately, barriers do exist which prevent children from achieving their full potential. It is the responsibility of all those who come into contact with children to ensure that they feel valued and valuable. It is important that children are both heard and seen to be heard. This may be achieved in individual and group situations and also through more formal arrangements such as a school council approach.

ISSUES OF INCLUSION

There is a great deal of discussion at the moment about the issue of inclusion. I think that it is important to spend some time considering a definition of inclusion. A real fear exists amongst teachers that they will be expected to teach and achieve good results from a wide range of children with an even wider range of special needs within mainstream classrooms without adequate support or appropriate training. Although the theme running through this book is that it is important to enable all children to feel included in the classroom situation and in the school, the role of targeted training and support has also been acknowledged. The book has concentrated mainly on

47

ways to include children with emotional, behavioural and learning difficulties because this was the focus of the research project. However, there are many children in schools who also have physical needs which takes the debate about inclusion into a wider arena. As Low (1997, pp.72–3) argues, inclusion means more than the simple inclusion of disabled people in society, it is about inclusivism, which is a holistic and systemic body of ideas. It involves the deconstruction of traditional conceptions of disability. It is about remodelling the institutions of society so that discriminatory arrangements currently made by society are changed to meet the needs of disabled people. This means that rather than just including children in the existing school system, we need to take a look at what is happening in the wider school society and how it is organized in terms of meeting the needs of all of its community, because as Low says: 'An environment which accommodates the needs of disabled people accommodates the needs of all.'

Chapter 10

Evaluation and conclusion

Initially, I began to develop a more reflective approach to teaching and learning in my classroom as a result of my search for ways to support children with special educational needs. During my analysis of children's views about our reflection time I realized that I was entering into their world in a way that had previously not been possible. I gradually gained an insight into how the children were feeling and I believe that the communication between us improved as a result of this experience. Although the initial ideas about reflection were mine, the children gradually moved away from my agenda and began to develop relevant aspects of the work for themselves. An important feature of professional reflective practice is that there is someone who is able to act as an agent in order to facilitate this development. It is difficult to be reflective by oneself within the context of personal and professional development and in the case of adults, a professional mentor or critical friend is able to perform this role. In the case of children, the candle used during reflection time acts as an initial focus or development agent for this purpose. The ensuing circle time enables the children further to develop their thoughts and to act as facilitators for each other.

The use of reflection time in the classroom has given a firm identity to an approach to teaching that is based on cooperation, respect, trust, independence and interdependence. A reflective approach to teaching and learning has many educational uses and it has been instrumental in improving the learning behaviour of many children. The approach has provided a medium for the development of spiritual, moral, social and cultural development and has brought a 'different' kind of atmosphere to the classroom. The spiritual aspect of the reflective approach has meant that children have been given time to think more deeply about important past and present events in their lives. It has also enabled them to develop confidence to discuss and to explore the difficult questions that may face them in their future lives. The use of a reflective approach has lead to the development of projects such as 'Boys Who Dance' and a mentoring system for young children. The mentoring system has in turn brought in children from other classes, which has resulted in a stronger community feeling. Inevitably the approach has enabled children who may have felt excluded in the past to become included in the education process in a more meaningful way. This is not only relevant in terms of special educational needs; a reflective approach also has potential relevance for all of the children and adults within a school. All of the children are able to benefit from the approach because overall there is less time spent on dealing with difficult situations and therefore there is less disruption to their education. When less time is allocated to dealing with disturbance, more time can be dedicated to the curriculum. Adults are able to benefit from the approach in a number of ways. As a result of the reflective approach, the day becomes less stressful for the adult workers and during reflection time they are able to share some time out with children. They will find themselves in a personal and professional development situation, which can lead to increased knowledge about children's development and learning. The fact that children are able to perform the role of mentors for each other indicates that they have embraced the concept of active reflective practice. I believe that as adults, we can learn from the children and become deeper and more effective reflective practitioners. I believe that the key to the development of successful reflective approaches to teaching and learning lies in a commitment to such an approach, combined with a willingness to learn alongside children in an open and honest way.

PART TWO

Appendices

Appendix 1

The Reflection Project

Background to the project school

The project school is a small infant and nursery school serving children from the age of three to seven, when they transfer to the junior school, which is located on the top floor of the same Victorian building. At the time of the project there were four full-time classes, with five classes during the summer term and a 25-place nursery unit. The complement of teachers consisted of head teacher, four/five full time teachers, including the deputy head and two job-share teachers, two full-time nursery nurses and one special needs support assistant who was also a qualified nursery nurse. During the project year, many other adults also came into contact with the children through the course of the day. These included the secretary, the site manager, domestic and cleaning staff and a group of people linked to outside agencies, such as the nurse, outreach teacher, emotional and behavioural support teacher and a teacher of deaf children from the Sensory Support Team. The school is located at the end of a cul-de-sac in a small ex-mining town on the Nottinghamshire and Derbyshire border. As in many such towns in Britain with similar industrial pasts, life is not easy for many of the inhabitants. Naturally, practical survival rather than spiritual reflection is the order of the day. The community is very supportive of the school, but conflict is nevertheless present. There is conflict between children, conflict between families and inevitably sometimes there is conflict with and within the school. Conflict resolution is a strong feature of the school day. Consequently, I have worked closely with groups of six- and seven-year-olds to develop strategies to deal with difficult situations.

Background to the Reflection Project

METHODOLOGY

The nature of enquiry into the role of reflection in the learning of young children led to the adoption of the action research method because: 'action research is appropriate whenever specific knowledge is required for a specific problem in a specific situation; or when a new approach is to be grafted onto an existing system' (Cohen and Manion, 1998, p. 194). I used the case study method based on participant observation as a methodological approach in the Reflection Project. I accept that there are problems of a subjective and idiosyncratic nature associated with this approach to educational research (Cohen and Manion, 1998, p. 123). However, the research data collected as a result of the approach are more accessible to a wider audience and therefore have more value in terms of direct interpretation and influence over changing everyday educational practice. The research for the Reflection Project was carried out over four terms during the academic years 1997-8 and 1998-9. Throughout the project I worked closely with a skilled and dedicated special needs support assistant who was also a qualified nursery nurse. We discussed strategies and worked out solutions together; we supported each other sharing the stress and strains of everyday life in the classroom. The first part of the project, or phase 1, took place during the summer term 1998, and involved a class of six- and seven-year-olds. These children had already begun to explore the possibilities of using a 'candle time' to look at and to change some of their more negative behaviour. A number of the children involved in phase 1 were

experiencing emotional and behavioural difficulties and two children in particular had severe speech problems; however, I felt that all of the children needed 'time out' during the busy day. Phase 2 of the project took place during the autumn, spring and summer terms of 1998-9 and involved children with similar backgrounds to those in phase 1. A number of children could not stay on task for any length of time and the development of speaking and listening skills was a priority for us all. Phase 2 of the project records the deeper development of a reflective approach with a class of Year 1 and Year 2 children who took the project into a different direction altogether. Many of the children in both phases of the project were experiencing a range of learning and emotional difficulties, which were set against a background of strategies for raising standards and target-setting. The development of the government's literacy and numeracy strategies was in full flow and a new curriculum was on the horizon. It was obvious that pressure and stress were building on teachers, children and their families to 'achieve, achieve, achieve'. The children's reactions to the Reflection Project were collected on tape at various times throughout the school day. Sometimes the children talked immediately after the reflection session had taken place and sometimes they talked spontaneously at other times about the various aspects of the project. They also used circle time to discuss each other's behaviour. After some of the reflection sessions and with the permission of the children, I passed around a small tape recorder. Sometimes the children would talk about how they felt about reflection and sometimes they would talk about what they had been thinking during the time that the candle was burning and the music was playing. All of the children's names have been changed in this book.

Reflection's good because I can think about my work instead of talking to other people. When we do reflection, when you close your eyes and think about something if you don't want to tell nobody at the end you don't have to.

Chloe

I like reflection because it is nice and calm. You think it in your head but when the candle goes off sometimes we tell people what we thought about.

Lisa

This decision to speak was very much their own. I found many benefits from this approach but I will let you make up your own minds when you read some of the children's comments. I have always focused on the spiritual, moral, social and cultural development of the children in my care. I have often used candles as a teaching aid to calm children and to prepare them for discussion time. Therefore, it has been a natural development for those two aspects of my practice to come together to form the basis of a research project. As my work in this area developed I felt that there was a need to explore the links between reflection and language development. A large number of my children were struggling to express their thoughts. I believed that, given time to think about what they wanted to say and a method through which they could express these thoughts, the children's language development would improve.

When the candle comes on you close your eyes and you think about something and it's nice and calm and if you're calm you can get a picture in your head about what you were thinking about.

Lisa

I also knew, as a result of my own training and experience, that this language development should in turn lead to an improvement in academic and social skills.

At the beginning of the research project I was a little uncertain about what I wanted to achieve other than responding to the difficulties that many of my children were experiencing. What actually happened, however, was that I was allowed a glimpse into the world of children and what they were thinking, which has led to a greater understanding on my behalf about what learning was taking place. I began to develop a greater sensitivity towards their feelings in a way that I had not really consciously considered before this time. I began to understand better what is meant by personal, emotional, cultural, social and moral development in a way that was both exciting and humbling for me. As for the children I will let them speak for themselves. All that I can do is to cast an experienced 'teacher-like' eye over what they are saying to try and make some sense of what we are doing to the children in our classrooms. A great deal of thought needs to go into the type of curriculum we offer to our children. In fact how often are the children, who are indeed the customers within schools, ever listened to or consulted with regard to what is taught and how that content is delivered? I have tried to listen to children and to give them room for the expression and autonomy that I believe should be the right of every child.

REFLECTION AND CRITICAL FRIENDSHIP

Reflection, as an aid to professional development, has been used in schools at an adult level for many years. The teacher as a reflective practitioner has been at the centre of a number of professional development programmes. A necessary condition for the development of the reflective professional has been a significant other, a mentor, and/or a critical friend who is also a supportive friend. The role of the critical friend, as I understand it, is to provide a focus for personal and professional development, an interactive sounding board for the developing practitioner. This is often the system found at the centre of induction programmes, although the format also has relevance for lifelong learning and development. Day et al. (1998, p.156) have defined the potential of critical friendship as: 'a means of establishing links with one or more colleagues to assist in the process of learning and change so that ideas, perceptions, values and understandings may be shared through the mutual disclosure of feelings, hopes and fears'.

I have developed a reflection time as part of my reflective approach. This is a time where children sit around a candle as music is playing and afterwards they have the option to share their thoughts during a circle time. Therefore, in the classroom situation, the candle becomes a focus for the children and the circle time allows space for the 'mutual disclosure of feelings, hopes and fears'.

At reflection you turn the lights off and look at the candles and then it makes you think if you close your eyes.

Josie

Reflection's all about when we look at the candle and turn off the lights and think how the day's been.

Lisa

The circle of children has taken over the role of the critical friends and eventually some of the children have become mentors for each other. The development of a reflection time has opened up so many other opportunities for development not only in my classroom but also throughout the rest of the school. The combination of the candle and the music also leads to a special feeling that awakens a sense of mystery in the children. Hay and Nye (1998) define this sense of mystery when they describe a child's sense of mystery being awakened by simple events such as the flame from a match or water coming out of the tap (p. 67). As a result of their work on the Children's Spirituality Project at Nottingham University, Hay and Nye found that children are capable of having profound beliefs and meaningful experience from an early age.

MENTORING AND DANCE

The children who have been involved in changing their behaviour through reflection have also taken on board a mentoring system.

In our class we have mentors to make sure that we be good cos a mentor mean you can be more better and be good.

Arron

We have mentors in our class for when people come from other classes and they are naughty and they can stop Billy and Neil from being bad.

Lisa

Billy and Neil were children from another class who joined the project class for short periods of time. The development of a mentoring system, which is described in greater detail elsewhere in the book, meant that children in another class who were suffering from similar difficulties to children in the project class have been included in the project.

> When Neil was sitting nicely and looking at the candle I was looking at the candle as well and Neil started to be nice and good to people. When Billy came in he was scrappy then when you lit the candle he sat nicely, then when it was the end of reflection, we talked and because looking at the candle it changes you.

Chloe

> When Neil first came into the classroom he used to be scrappy and then he used to go under tables and in his classroom, but when I took him down to our class, he was nice and calm.

Ryan

The development of a reflective and inclusive approach meant that a dance project, which was also aimed at increasing the involvement of boys, took on a greater significance.

EXPRESSING THEMSELVES

A major source of frustration for me at the time of the project was watching the way that many of the children struggled to find the words to express themselves. This begged the question: Did they actually understand the curriculum content and just not have the language to express this understanding, or did they not have any understanding? Whichever case was true, it would and should not only affect my planning and assessment procedures but my whole approach to teaching. I had come across this situation before when I worked with children for whom English was an additional language, yet I was less prepared for such a situation when working with children for whom English was the only language. Some of the children in the group suffered from pronounced speech difficulties that consequently led to a lack of confidence when speaking in front of others.

> My name Nicola and when, em, there, when we have deflection, em we durn the lights off.

Nicola

Some of the children seemed to be 'vocabulary starved' and did not have access to a wide range of stimulating and expressive language. Whatever the reasons were for the existence of such a situation, and this book is not about such analysis, it is certain that a significant situation existed which affected the achievement of a group of children in an adverse way.

CHALLENGING BEHAVIOUR

During the past years in my teaching it has become more and more obvious to me that there has been an increasing need to find new ways to help children to learn. More and more demands on teachers in terms of fulfilling curriculum orders and meeting new targets in the endless battle to raise standards has meant a decreasing emphasis on understanding how children are actually learning as opposed to developing teaching strategies to deal with an ever-increasing content. As Acker (1999, p. 4) discovered in her research into the life of an English primary school, primary teaching is incredibly difficult work affected by temperaments, abilities, interruptions, moods, time of the day and even the weather! There is little doubt that many teachers, no matter how experienced or talented, find the behaviour of some of the children in their care to be challenging. This has been the case for myself and many of my colleagues. I know that I have targets to reach and deadlines to meet but sometimes my children have small sympathy for that and instead they wish to react, disrupt and destroy some of my well-laid plans. Oh, how I hate all that wasted time spent on planning something that I cannot teach because someone in my class has an alternative agenda to mine! This is also frustrating for the majority in the class who want to learn and who although good-natured become increasingly frustrated by the interruptions.

West and Sammons (1996) conducted research into six inner city infant schools and found that the teaching and learning processes, particularly with those children with additional learning needs, had been profoundly affected by the introduction of the National Curriculum. They found that teachers felt under tremendous pressure and complained of lack of time to teach children with extra needs. They found that all of the children and particularly bright children suffered because the teachers spent so much time dealing with children with additional needs.

RELIGIOUS EDUCATION COORDINATOR

Another reason for needing to define a particular approach to teaching was that I found myself in the role of religious education coordinator. In my experience it is often the case that this is not a popular role to embrace. I must admit I felt that I was not looking forward to leading others in such an area. However, what the situation did do was to focus my mind on how difficult it was to teach religious education in any sort of meaningful way to such young children. I had always worked in inner city schools before my present post, where many of the children belonged to religious communities reflecting a cross-section of world religions. I now found myself in a situation where this was definitely not the case. Therefore, all of my teaching about world religions had to be carried out 'second-hand'. I was aware not only that the children were struggling to understand the content of my religious education lessons, but that I also had to provide some sort of lead in this curriculum area. Hence the need to construct a platform from which the children could develop some appreciation of why religions exist and why people worship. There was also a need to create a similar kind of ambience within the classroom environment that could be found in places of worship in order to make the teaching more relevant. The nearest I could get to this was a reflection time.

> When it's reflection, I think about Buddhas and it's calm. When we do reflection we're all calm and then we turn the lights on and we do some work then we can we do it properly because we've done reflection because we thought about it before we did it. When the temple music is on we can think about Buddha and when we looked in this book and we saw a temple.
>
> **Lisa**

It is the same principle as creating an appropriate setting for a science lesson for example, in terms of providing the correct equipment, relevant resources, organization and content. If, for instance, artefacts were to be effectively explored, then the setting had to be different. If a discussion about why people pray was to take place, then a suitable atmosphere needed to exist within the classroom to make the discussion more relevant.

> The candle's on and you can think about religion because you've just looked at the candle, that's why you can think about it. When I do reflection I think about when the candle's on I think about what the day's been like and when we've done religious education like when we did about Jesus I thought about that.
>
> **Lisa**

> When the candle's on and when it blows out and you can do some religion afterwards and you can think about religion.
>
> **Zara**

These are some of the reasons for the emergence of a reflection time in my own classroom; however, I don't think that I actually realized at the time that this was just the beginning of an exciting and innovative learning project.

Reflection as an approach to teaching and learning

> I like reflection because when you think and you can think about what you want and then after you've done and you can do your work better if you've had time to think.
>
> **Ryan**

The original reason for the Reflection Project was to help children to think, talk and learn in an enjoyable and rewarding way. It was not connected consciously with the school's target-setting agenda, although eventually it did enter these realms.

I was initially seeking an approach to teaching and learning that would benefit the school community, not only in terms

of language development, but also in the management of unacceptable behaviour, and what I actually discovered was an approach that also contributed to personal, emotional and spiritual development. My initial response to the problems the children were experiencing was to set aside some time in the busy day in order to allow the children some time to think. I felt that I was placing demands on the children, both academically and socially, without allowing them adequate time to consider these demands. This took me into the realms of research into children's thinking.

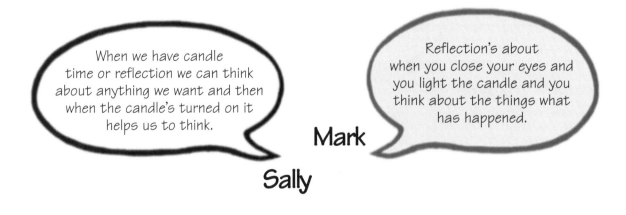

When we have candle time or reflection we can think about anything we want and then when the candle's turned on it helps us to think.

Sally

Mark

Reflection's about when you close your eyes and you light the candle and you think about the things what has happened.

Reflection time: time out to think

This 'time out to think' was also for my benefit; there always seemed to be so much happening that I felt that I needed to stop and think or, as it became known to the group, to stop and reflect. This book tells the story of the development of that time out to think, into an action research project called 'Reflection Time'. At this point I would like to explain the term 'reflection' within the context of this project. For those involved in the project, reflection simply meant time out to think. In terms of spirituality and children it translates into a situation where the time out becomes a 'special time', which also brings a different special dimension to the work in progress; this time for reflection is now firmly ingrained into our classroom culture.

Well reflection means you come to the best part of your life because that's the only thing that clears out your head. — Trevor

I like reflection because when I've had a hard day at school, when it's reflection I get to calm down. — Sally

Success criteria

As the research project developed it became clear that the successful reflective classroom should have certain identifiable features. These features have been identified in this section, although the success criteria have not been placed in any particular order.

ATMOSPHERE

Within the reflective classroom, the atmosphere is calm and if situations do arise, then the children are able to deal with most of them without any adult intervention. This is especially important at times such as the literacy hour when it is necessary for groups to work independently and to remain on task for an extended period of time.

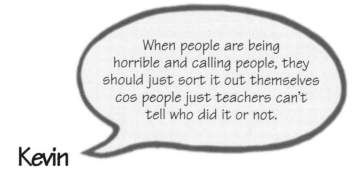

When people are being horrible and calling people, they should just sort it out themselves cos people just teachers can't tell who did it or not. — Kevin

RELATIONSHIPS

The quality of relationships within the reflective classroom can be measured by the way in which the occupants speak to each other, show respect for each other and understand each other's needs.

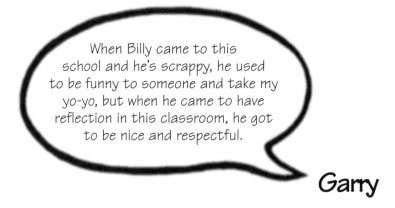

When Billy came to this school and he's scrappy, he used to be funny to someone and take my yo-yo, but when he came to have reflection in this classroom, he got to be nice and respectful.

Garry

Teamwork

The children and the adults in the team are supportive of each other. There is an understanding of the importance of the concept of inclusion and a commitment to looking after each other, which extends to others outside the classroom situation.

SUPPLY TEACHERS

The way in which a class works when the class teacher is not present is usually quite a good indication of their commitment to a reflective and cooperative approach. Although there will always potentially be incidents in this situation, supply teachers made favourable comments during the project year about the behaviour of the children in the project class.

Results

Academic achievement can be measured using data from baseline assessments and target projections; in some cases higher results than those predicted were achieved by children in the project class whose learning behaviour had been improved as a result of a reflective approach.

Mentoring and dance projects

Within the Reflection Project there were two 'mini-projects' which focused on mentoring and dance. The aim of both of the projects was specifically to raise the achievement of boys in the class. I tentatively introduced mentoring to the class as I thought that there could be a number of problems inherent in such a scheme with very young children. I still feel that as an approach, mentoring has to be sensitively handled, modified and reviewed; however, it is worthwhile to attempt to build a support system which involves the children themselves.

The dance project took 6 months of hard work and exploration of team-building and gender issues. There was a great deal of fun, exercise and enjoyment as well as exploration of feelings and the development of enough confidence to perform in front of an audience. I believe that as a result of the dance project, the self-esteem of many of the children was raised, which meant that they tended to become more involved in a wider range of classroom activities. This was particularly the case for a small group of boys who were previously reluctant to take part in classroom work of *any* nature. The actual dance performance, which was incidentally of secondary importance to the development work, took place at the end of the project year, which meant that the wider school community was able to share in the children's achievements.

Carl

Whole school improvement

Whole school improvement can be a gradual process dependent upon a number of factors such as the existing school culture, style of leadership, size of school and the age and aspirations of staff. However, if the school as a whole is spending too much time and energy dealing with disruption and conflict there will be less scope for focusing on other important issues. Therefore any approach, such as a reflective approach, that minimizes time-wasting must contribute to school improvement.

The book contains guidelines for those of you who wish to become involved in work of this type which, if approached with sensitivity and expectation, can provide real support for children with special educational needs and those who find life in the classroom so difficult to cope with. I hope that if you do try some of the methods suggested in this book it will bring similar feelings of peace and tranquillity to your situation, even if only for a short and reflective time!

Appendix 2

Bibliography

Sandra Acker, *The Realities of Teachers' Work*, Cassell, 1999.

Louis Cohen and Lawrence Manion, *Research Methods in Education*, Routledge, 1998.

William Damon and Anne Colby, 'Education and moral commitment', *Journal of Moral Education*, Vol.25, No.1, pp. 32–35, 1996.

Christopher Day, Carol Hall and Patrick Whitaker, *Developing Leadership in Primary Schools*, Paul Chapman, 1998.

DES, *Discipline in Schools*, *The Elton Report*, HMSO, 1989.

Robert Fisher, *Teaching Children to Think*, Blackwell, 1990.

David Hay and Rebecca Nye, *The Spirit of the Child*, HarperCollins, 1998.

Robert Jackson, *Religious Education: an Interpretative Approach*, Hodder & Stoughton, 1997.

Jane Kenway and Lindsay Fitzclarence, 'Masculinity, violence and schooling: Challenging "Poisonous pedagogies"', *Gender and Education*, Vol.9, No.1, pp.71–9, 1997.

Colin Low, 'Is inclusivism possible?', *European Journal of Special Needs,* Vol.12, No.1, pp. 71–9, 1997.

Sandra McNamara and Gill Moreton, *Changing Behaviour*, David Fulton, 1995.

Carolyn Webster-Stratton and Martin Herbert, *Troubled Families – Problem Children: Working With Parents: A Collaborative Approach*, Wiley, 1995.

Anne West and Pat Sammons, 'Children with and without "Additional Educational Needs" at Key Stage 1 in six inner city schools – teaching and learning processes and policy implications', *British Educational Research Journal,* Vol.22, No.1, pp.125–33, 1996.

William David Wills, *Throw Away Thy Rod*, Victor Gollancz, 1960.

Appendix 3

Suitable music for reflection time

Original soundtrack recording, *Cats,* The Really Useful Group Ltd, 1998

Track 7   'Memory'

Enya, *Shepherd Moons*, Warner Music Ltd, 1991

Track 1   'Shepherd Moons'

Track 3   'How Can I Keep From Singing'

Track 5   'Angeles'

Track 6   'No Holly for Miss Quinn'

Track 12   'Smaointe'

Labi Siffre, *So Strong*, China Records Ltd, 1988

Track 6   'Something Inside So Strong'

Various artists, *New Pure Moods,* Virgin Records Ltd, 1997

CD One

Track 2   Enigma, 'Return to Innocence'

Track 3   Sacred Spirit, 'Yeha-Noha' (Wishes of Peace and Happiness)

Track 4   Deep Forest, 'Sweet Lullaby'

Track 9   Elton John, 'Song for Guy'

Track 10   Michael Nyman, 'The Heart Asks Pleasure First' (theme from *The Piano*)

Track 16   John Williams, 'Cavatina' (theme from *The Deerhunter*)

Track 18   Fleetwood Mac, 'Albatross'

Various artists, *One World*, BMG International Entertainment UK and Ireland Ltd, 1998

CD Two

Track 11   Jing Long Uen and Song Huei Liou with Buddhism Chanting Group Hanshan Temple

Track 12   Sacred Spirit, 'Yeha-Noha' (Wishes of Peace and Prosperity)

Various artists, *Sacred Spirit: Chants and Dances of the Native Americans*, Virgin Records Ltd, 1994

Track 7   'Yeha-Noha' (Wishes of Peace and Prosperity)

Track 9   'Heya-Hee'

Simon and Garfunkel, *The Definitive Simon and Garfunkel*, Sony Music Entertainment Ltd, 1991

Track 19   'Bridge over Troubled Water'

Various artists, *The Most Relaxing Classical Album in the World Ever*, EMI Records Ltd, 1997

CD One

Track 1   J.S. Bach, 'Air on the G String'

Track 3   Pachelbel, Canon

Track 5   Satie, Gymnopèdie No. 1

Track 9   Debussy, 'Clair de Lune'

Track 10   Mendelssohn, Violin Concerto in E Minor

Track 11   Saint-Saëns, 'The Swan'

Track 15   Elgar, 'Nimrod' Variation

CD Two

Track 2   Albinoni, Adagio

Track 5   Massenet, 'Meditation'

Track 6   Beethoven, 'Moonlight' Sonata

Track 9   Mozart, Clarinet Concerto

Track 16   Rodrigo, *Concierto de Aranjuez*

Track 17   Barber, Adagio

Track 18   Bizet, Entra'cte to Act III (Carmen)

The Spirit of Tranquility Harmonium, BMG Entertainment International Ltd UK and Ireland, 1998

CD One

Track 1   'Rose' (theme from *Titanic*)

Track 2   'Morning Mist'

Track 3   'Mountain Spring'

Track 4   'Voice of Calm'

Track 9   'Healing Hands'

Track 12   'Magic Canvas'

CD Two

Track 7   'Peace Chant'

Track 8   'Andalusian Shores'

Track 11   'Romeo and Juliet'

Appendix 4

The Red and Green Project

Background to the Red and Green Story

The stimulus for the Red and Green Story came from some work undertaken during a topic called 'People'. The topic enabled the class to consider issues of diversity, both within the classroom and the local community. Bullying, name-calling and racial abuse were discussed at length. During a drama session later in the term we discussed how some people are not allowed to mix if they are different. The children were divided into two groups and not allowed to work together for the session. They chose the colours red and green to differentiate themselves. The groups then began to identify with the two colours and the people within their own particular groups.

The children had also used the book *Tusk Tusk* by David McKee (Arrow, 1983) during the previous term and had discussed the issues arising from the book. The song 'Something Inside So Strong' by Labi Siffre was used as a further aid to understanding the quite complex issues engendered by such work. We discussed the lyrics of the song and I explained how it had been written about the apartheid situation in South Africa. The story of the Red and Green people began to evolve gradually into a project which then involved other staff, children in the school and parents. The children used equipment around them, such as large building blocks, to construct barriers and to examine the problems caused by the barriers. They also decided to build homes for themselves and their families and it was their decision to elect a leader, which they did using pieces of paper! Meetings were also held to resolve conflict situations, e.g. writing to the President to complain about the treatment of the Green people. In the end it turned out that all of the people wanted to live together and the blame was put on the President (who was female) for keeping them apart. When the Red people finally released the Green people from the jail, the President was imprisoned. However, the people decided to give the President another chance. The children, who were also dealing with issues of social justice and equality at a mature level, made all of these decisions. At the end of the drama everyone joined together to sing the song 'Something Inside So Strong' and when questioned the Red people said that they wanted to stay on the island and they did not want to return to their own island. It turned out that they themselves had been persecuted by the Blue people and were forced to leave. It almost ends in true fairy tale style with them all living happily ever after, although it would be interesting to follow the story and to see how the two groups coped with life together.

Welcome to Greenland

Once upon a time there was an island. Green people lived on the island. They went about their daily business. One day a boat arrived on the far side of the island. The boat was carrying Red people. The Red people brought big bricks with them. They landed and began to settle on the island. They built homes with their bricks and their President built a large palace. They also built a brick wall across the island to keep all of the other people out. The wall stopped the Green people getting water and some of their food. One night when everyone was fast asleep, something happened.

One of the Green people couldn't sleep because he was very hungry. He went for a walk and he came to the brick wall. It was very high so he couldn't climb over it but he found a loose brick and he climbed through the wall. One of the Red people was out for a walk; he met the Green person and they made friends. The Green person took the Red person to the other side of the island.

The Red person was shocked when he saw how hungry and miserable the Green people were. The Red person took the Green people to meet the Red people. They sat down and had a meal together.

After the Green people had returned to their side of the island the Red people had a meeting. They decided to write letters to the President but when she read them she ripped them up and warned the Red people not to mix with the Green people. Life carried on until one day the Green people decide that they had had enough and they marched to the Palace. The President and her troops overpowered the Green people and put them into a dark dungeon.

The President told the Red people to forget about the Green people but the Red people decided to release them. They threw the President and her troops into the jail instead.

They set off together to knock down the wall and to build new homes. The President and her troops wanted to join in and THE PEOPLE decided to include them. When they had finished building they all joined together to sing the song 'Something Inside So Strong' by Labi Siffre.

Issues arising from the Red and Green drama

+ Where did the Red and Green people come from?

+ Had they been victims of persecution in their own land?

+ Who had the power, was it the Red President, the Red people, or the Green people?

+ Who decided that a wall should be built in the first place?

+ Why didn't the Red people realize that they would cause suffering by their actions?

+ When the Red and Green people meet each other, what differences do they notice about each other? Were there any differences amongst the Red people themselves and similarly the Green people?

+ Did they all get on well together or were there any problems?

+ What would the Red people have to do in order to mix with the Green people?

+ How far were they prepared to go?

- When the Green people failed to effect any change by peaceful means were they justified in marching on the President's palace?

- How did the Red people rectify the situation?

- Should the President have been given another chance after all of the things she did?

- Why were the people singing 'Something Inside So Strong'?

- Why didn't the Red people return to their own land?

- How could the bricks be used to benefit all of the people?

- Did they really live happily ever after?

- Which other factors, apart from skin colour, could cause such division amongst people?

- Who should be the new president and how would a new president be chosen?

- Was a president necessary?

- Should it be a Green person?

- How much power should the new president have?

- How much power should the people have?

- What about the individual?

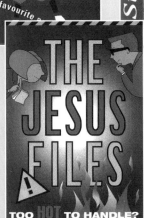